Senses

Hearing
in Living Things

Karen Hartley, Chris Macro and Philip Taylor

Heinemann
LIBRARY

312

First published in Great Britain by Heinemann Library,
Halley Court, Jordan Hill, Oxford OX2 8EJ
a division of Reed Educational and Professional Publishing Ltd.
Heinemann is a registered trademark of Reed Educational & Professional Publishing Ltd.

OXFORD MELBOURNE AUCKLAND
JOHANNESBURG BLANTYRE GABORONE
IBADAN PORTSMOUTH (NH) USA CHICAGO

Designed by Celia Floyd
Illustrated by Alan Fraser
Originated by Ambassador Litho Ltd, UK
Printed in Hong Kong / China

05 04 03 02 01
10 9 8 7 6 5 4 3 2 1

ISBN 0 431 09728 3
This title is also available in a hardback library edition (ISBN 0 431 09721 6).

British Library Cataloguing in Publication Data

Hartley, Karen
    Hearing in living things. – (Senses)
    1. Hearing – Juvenile literature
    2. Sense organs – Juvenile literature
    I. Title II. Macro, Chris III. Taylor, Philip

Acknowledgements

The Publishers would like to thank the following for permission to reproduce photographs:

BBC p.26; Bruce Coleman: Jane Burton p.16, Johnny Johnson p.28; Corbis/Eye Ubiquitous: Robert & Linda Mostyn p.14; FLPA: Ian Cartwright p.21; Heinemann: Gareth Boden p.4, p.5, p.6, p.7, p.8, p.10, p.12, p.13, p.24, p.25; Image Bank: Anne Rippy p.11; Oxford Scientific Films: Kathie Atkinson p.18, Marty Cordano p.23; Pictor International p.17, p.19, p.20, p.22; Planet Earth Pictures p.27; Sally Greenhill p.15; Tony Stone: Eastcott/Momatiuk p.29.

Cover photograph reproduced with permission of Oxford Scientific Films and Gareth Boden.

Many thanks to the teachers and pupils of Abbotsweld Primary School, Harlow.

Every effort has been made to contact copyright holders of any material reproduced in this book. Any omissions will be rectified in subsequent printings if notice is given to the Publisher.

For more information about Heinemann Library books, or to order, please telephone +44 (0)1865 888066, or send a fax to +44 (0)1865 314091. You can visit our web site at www.heinemann.co.uk

Any words appearing in the text in bold, **like this**, are explained in the Glossary.

Contents

What are your senses?

People and animals have senses to help them find out about the world. You use your senses to feel, see, hear, taste and smell. Your senses can warn you of danger.

Your senses are very important to you and other animals every day. This book is about your sense of hearing. You are going to find out how it works and what you use it for.

What do you use to hear?

You use your ears to hear with. You have two ears and they are on the sides of your head. This helps you to hear sounds from all directions, without turning round.

Your ears hear sounds all the time. You can usually tell which direction a sound is coming from. It is hard to stop hearing sounds as you cannot close your ears.

How do you hear?

Sounds are made when things **vibrate**.
Different vibrations make loud sounds, soft
sounds, **high sounds** and **low sounds**.
You can hear most vibrations.

Inside an ear is a small stretched piece of skin, which is called an eardrum. It senses the vibrations. Messages are sent to the brain which tells you what the sounds are.

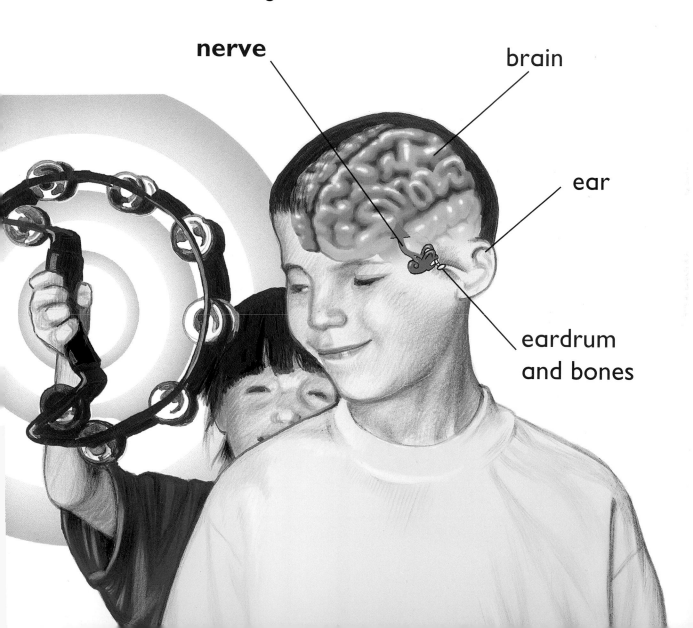

nerve

brain

ear

eardrum and bones

How does hearing help you?

If you listen carefully your ears can help you to keep safe. When you cross the road you need to listen for the sounds of traffic as well as look for it.

Your ears help you to learn. You have a **language** with words for everything you think of. It can be fun listening to stories and hearing about interesting things.

What do you use hearing for?

Your ears help you to find out about other people and what is going on around you. You can share secrets with a friend. You can listen to music you like.

You listen while you are watching television. If people you love are far away you can still hear their voices using the telephone. They can hear about what you have been doing.

What can happen?

People can become **deaf**. Young people can become deaf. People often become deaf when they grow old. Listening to loud noises for a long time can damage your ears.

Some deaf people use a **hearing aid** to hear better. Some use a sign **language** with their hands. Others watch lips moving to know what people are saying.

Do animals have ears?

Most animals have ears. Bats use their sense of hearing to catch flying **insects** to eat. The bats make tiny squeaky sounds. They hear the sounds bouncing back off the insects so they know where they are.

Frogs have ears. They can hear the sounds of animals which want to eat them. They can hear other frogs. They cannot hear anything else.

Other ways to hear sounds

Grasshoppers and crickets are **insects** which can hear sounds. Their ears are not on their heads. Some have ears on their knees. Some have ears on their sides.

Some spiders can hear very well. They have hairs on their legs. Large spiders have long hairs. Sounds make the hairs **vibrate** and the spiders hear them.

How do animals use hearing?

Many animals have to catch their food. The barn owl flies at night and listens very carefully. It can hear a mouse running in a field. It can catch it to eat.

Fish can hear sounds. They hear through their sides. Sound **vibrations** travel through water very well. Some **male** and **female** fish use sounds to find each other to **mate**.

Using hearing to stay safe

Some animals use their ears to sense if their enemies are close by. Rabbits have long ears. They can turn their ears towards sounds to hear them better.

The kangaroo rat has very good hearing. It lives in the desert and comes out at night. It can hear the tiny sound of the **scales** of a rattlesnake moving on the sand.

Investigating hearing

Sounds can travel through **solid** things like wood. Knock gently against a table. How does it sound? Put your ear against the table. Does it sound different now?

Wrap some elastic bands round an empty plastic tub. Use wide ones and narrow ones. Pluck them with your fingers. Which make **high sounds**? Which make **low sounds**?

Playing tricks on your ears

Have you seen a **ventriloquist**? They speak without moving their lips so you think it is the **dummy** talking. They can be very funny. Try to talk without moving your lips.

Some birds can **mimic** the way you speak. They do not understand the **language**. If you hear a mynah bird when you cannot see it, its voice sounds like a person speaking.

Did you know?

Elephants make very **low sounds** which travel a long way. Other elephants hear them far away. Elephants flap their huge ears to keep cool and not to hear better.

You cannot hear the low sounds the elephant makes. They are too low. Dogs can hear **high sounds** that you cannot hear. A dog whistle will sound silent to you.

Glossary

deaf   not being able to hear

dummy   a doll

female   a girl

hearing aid   a small box which makes sounds louder to help deaf people

high sounds   sounds like a small whistle or a scream

insects   small animals with six legs

language   the words that we use whenever we talk

low sounds   sounds like a big drum or thunder

male   a boy

mate   a male and a female join up to make babies

mimic   to copy

nerve   something that carries messages from the body to the brain

pinna   the part of the ear we see on the outside of the head

scales   small hard pieces of skin on snakes and fish

solid   all in one piece

ventriloquist   a person who pretends that a dummy can talk

vibrate   to move quickly backwards and forwards like a guitar string when it is played

Sense map

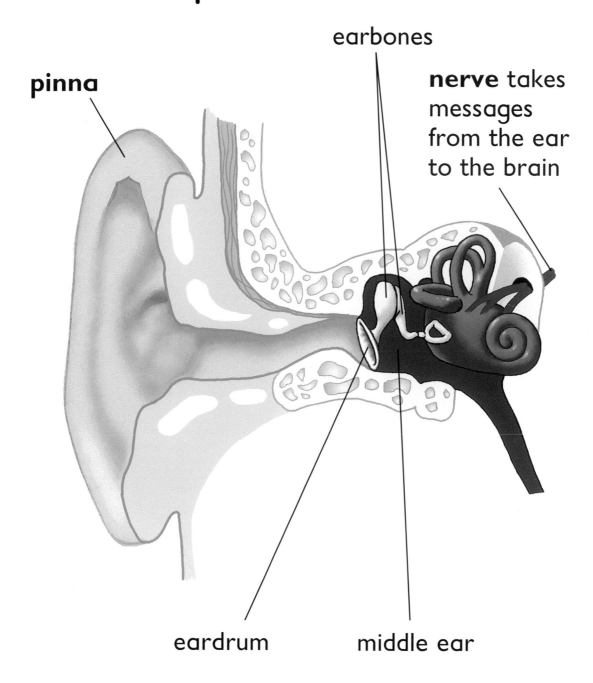

pinna

earbones

nerve takes messages from the ear to the brain

eardrum

middle ear

Index